SYMPHONY NO. 9
in Full Score

GUSTAV MAHLER

DOVER PUBLICATIONS, INC.

New York

This Dover edition, first published in 1993, is a republication of the edition originally published by Universal-Edition, Vienna, in 1912, as *Neunte Symphonie von Gustav Mahler. Partitur.* The footnote in the score has been newly translated, and a list of instruments and glossary of German terms have been provided.

Manufactured in the United States of America
Dover Publications, Inc., 31 East 2nd Street, Mineola, N.Y. 11501

Library of Congress Cataloging-in-Publication Data

Mahler, Gustav, 1860–1911.
   [Symphonies, no. 9]
   Symphony no. 9 / Gustav Mahler. — In full score.
   1 score.
   Reprint. Originally published: Vienna : Universal-Edition, 1912.
   ISBN 0-486-27492-6 (pbk.)
   1. Symphonies—Scores.
M1001.M21   no. 9 1993   92-42995
                                               CIP
                                                 M

CONTENTS

GLOSSARY OF GERMAN TERMS IN THE SCORE

3 fach geteilt, divided in three parts (voices)

3-taktig, three-measure phrase

aber ausdrucksvoll, but expressively

aber etwas schneller als das erstemal, but somewhat faster than at first

aber nicht schleppend, but not dragging

aber sehr hervortretend, but very prominent

aber viel langsamer als zu Anfang, but much slower than the opening

alle, tutti

allein, solo, alone

Allmählich, gradually

Allmählich an Ton gewinnend, gradually swelling the tone

Allmählich fliessender, gradually more flowing

allmählich übergehen zu Tempo I., Gradually return to Tempo I

am Steg, at the bridge

Anwachsend, rising up

ausdrucksvoll, expressively

Äusserst langsam, extremely slow

Bewegter, more animated

bis zum Schluss, to the end

Dämpfer ab, take mute off

Das Tempo so weit mässigen, als nötig, The tempo broader as necessary

deutlich, clearly

doch durchaus nicht eilend, but always without hurrying

doch nie überhetzt, yet without ever losing control

Einhaltend, restrained

ersterbend, dying away

Es dur, moll, E♭ major, minor

Etwas belebter, somewhat livelier

Etwas drängend, somewhat pressing

etwas eilend, somewhat hastened

Etwas fliessender, somewhat more flowing

Etwas frischer, somewhat livelier

etwas gehalten, held back a little

Etwas täppisch und sehr derb, somewhat clumsy and very coarse

Fernerhin mit Tempo I. bezeichnet, hereafter marked as Tempo I.

Flag. (auf der . . . Saite), harmonic (on the . . . string)

Flatterzunge, fluttertongue

Fliessend, flowing

Flott, buoyant

ganz langsam, very slow

Gehalten, held back

gestopft, gest., stopped

geteilt, get., divided (= divisi)

glänzend, brilliant

Griffbrett, fingerboard

grosser Ton, full tone

Hälfte, half

heftig ausbrechend, with a violent outburst

hervortretend, prominent

Höchste Kraft, greatest power

Im Tempo eines gemächlichen Ländlers, in a comfortable Ländler tempo

immer, always, still

Immer dasselbe Tempo, always the same tempo

immer gestopft, still stopped

in Tempo II (Walzer) übergehen, move to Tempo II. (Waltz)

keck, bold

klagend, lamenting

klingen lassen, let ring

lang gestrichen, long bows

lang gezogen, drawn out, spun out

langsam (wie vorher), slow (as before)

Leidenschaftlich, passionately

leise, soft

mit, with

mit Dämpfer, with mute

Mit grosser Empfindung, with great feeling

mit höchster Gewalt, with utmost force

mit inniger Empfindung, with heartfelt emotion

Mit Wut, with rage

natürlich, natural playing position

Nicht eilen (bis zum Schluss), without rushing (till the end)

nicht espress., no expression

Nicht mehr so langsam, no longer so slow

nicht schleppen, do not drag

nicht zu schnell, not too fast

nimmt, change to

noch breiter als zu Anfang, even broader than at the beginning

Noch etwas frischer, yet a bit more vigorously

Noch etwas lebhafter, somewhat livelier still

noch etwas zögernd, still somewhat hesitating

Nun etwas drängend, henceforth pressing the tempo somewhat

offen, open

ohne Ausdruck, without feeling

ohne Dämpfer, without mute

ohne Empfindung, without emotion

Plötzlich bedeutend langsamer, at once significantly slower

Plötzlich langsamer, All at once slower

Plötzlich sehr mässig und zurückhaltend,

suddenly very moderate and held back

Pult, stand, desk

S., Saite, string

Schalltr[ichter] auf, bells (of horns, etc.) held high

Schattenhaft, shadowy, indistinct

schmeichelnd, ingratiating, flattering

Schon ganz langsam, here, completely slow

Schon langsam, slow already

Schwebend, suspended

Schwerfällig, ponderous, heavy-footed

Sehr fliessend, very flowing

sehr gemächlich, very comfortable

sehr getragen, very solemn

Sehr mässigend, with great moderation

Sehr trotzig, very insolent

sehr weich, very soft

sehr weich hervortretend, prominent, yet very soft

sehr zart, very smooth (legato)

sehr zart, aber ausdrucksvoll, very tender, yet expressive

sehr zögernd, very hesitant

Sord[inen] (ab, auf), mute (on, off)

stark hervortretend, in marked prominence

stets breitester Strich!, steady, very broad bow strokes

stets grosser Ton, steady full tone

stets mit höchster Kraft, steadily with the utmost power

Stets sehr gehalten, held back steadily

Straffer in Tempo, stricter in tempo

unmerklich, imperceptibly

verklingend, fading away

viel Bogen, many bow strokes

weich geblasen, blown softly

Wie ein schwerer Kondukt, like a ponderous funeral procession

wie Fiedeln, like fiddles

Wie von (zu) Anfang, like the beginning

wie zuvor, as before

Wieder a Tempo, again a tempo

Wieder altes Tempo, again the former tempo

Wieder zurückhaltend, held back again

zart gesungen, gently, cantabile

zögernd, hesitating

zu 2 (3), both (all three) players

♩ *wie früher* ♩, ♩ = the earlier ♩

♪ *wie im letzten Takte die* ♩, ♪ = ♩ of previous measure

♩ *wie vorher* ♩, ♩ = preceding ♩

INSTRUMENTATION

Piccolo (Kleine Flöte; Kl. Fl.)
4 Flutes (Flöten; Fl.)
3 Oboes (Oboen; Ob.)
English Horn (Englischhorn; Englh.)
Clarinet in E ♭ (Klarinette in Es; Klar. in Es)
3 Clarinets in A, B ♭ (Klarinette; Klar. in A, B)
Bass Clarinet in B ♭ (Bassklarinette; B.-Klar. in B)
3 Bassoons (Fagotte; Fag.)
Contrabassoon [also doubles as 4th Bassoon] (Kontra-Fagott; K.-Fag.)

4 Horns in F (Hörner; Hr.)
3 Trumpets in F (Trompeten; Trp.)
3 Trombones (Posaunen; Pos.)
Tuba (Basstuba; Btb.)

Timpani (2 players) (Pauken; Pk.)
Glockenspiel (Glsp.)
3 low-pitched Bells (Tiefe Glocken); pitched:
Triangle (Triangel; Trgl.)
Cymbals (Becken; Beck.)
Tamtam (Tm.)
Bass Drum (Grosse Trommel; Gr. Tr.)
Snare Drum (Kleine Trommel; Kl. Tr.)

2 Harps (Harfen)

Violins I & II (Violinen; Vl.)
Violas (Viola; Vla.)
Cellos (Violoncell; Vlc.)
Basses (Kontrabass; Kb.)

I.

1

II.

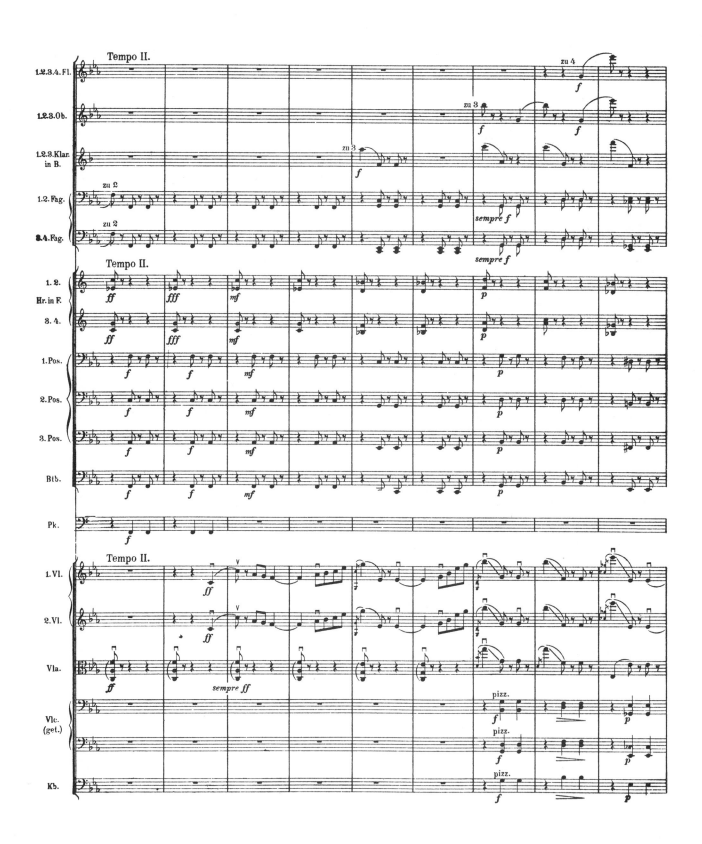

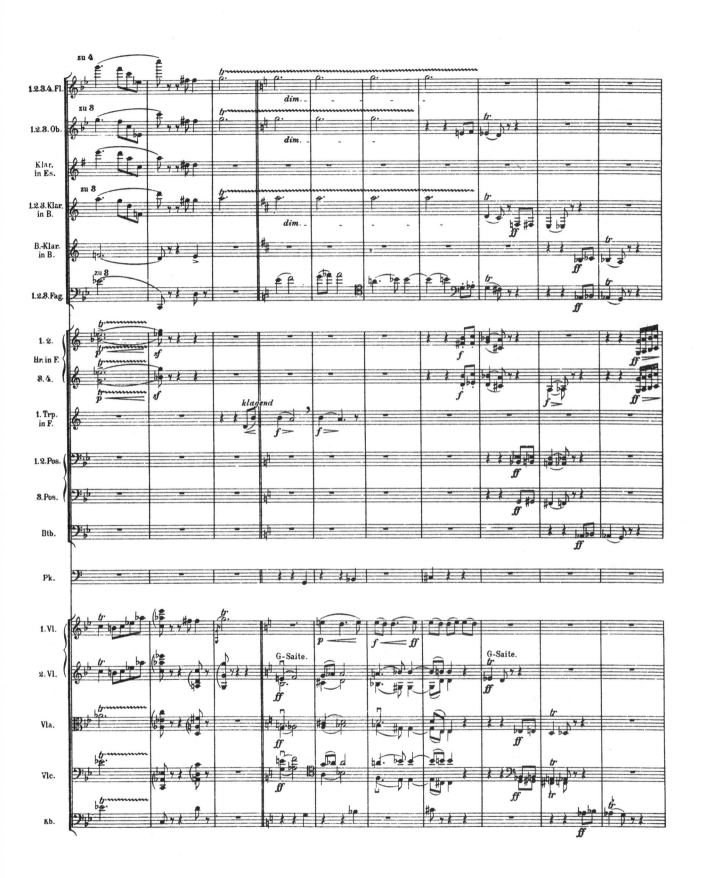

III. Rondo. Burleske.

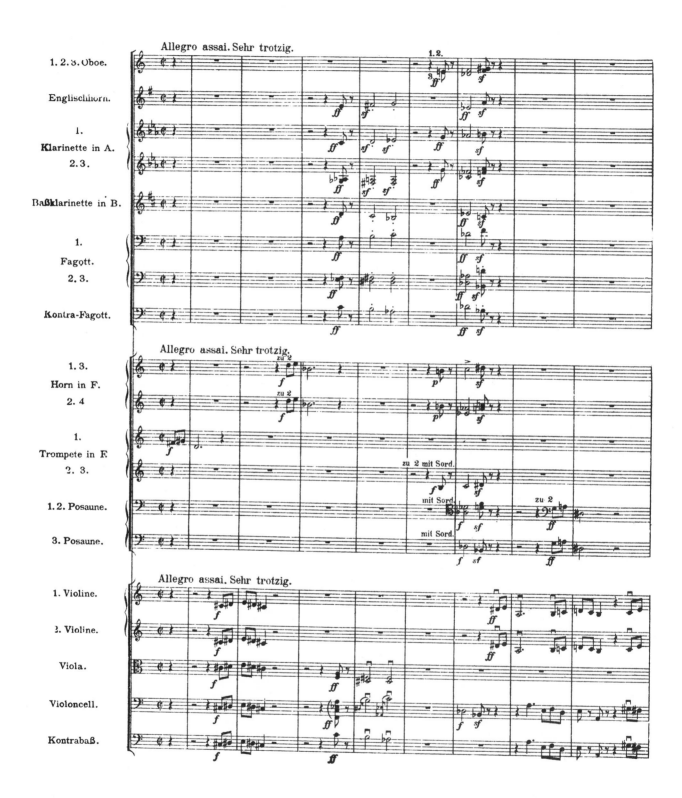

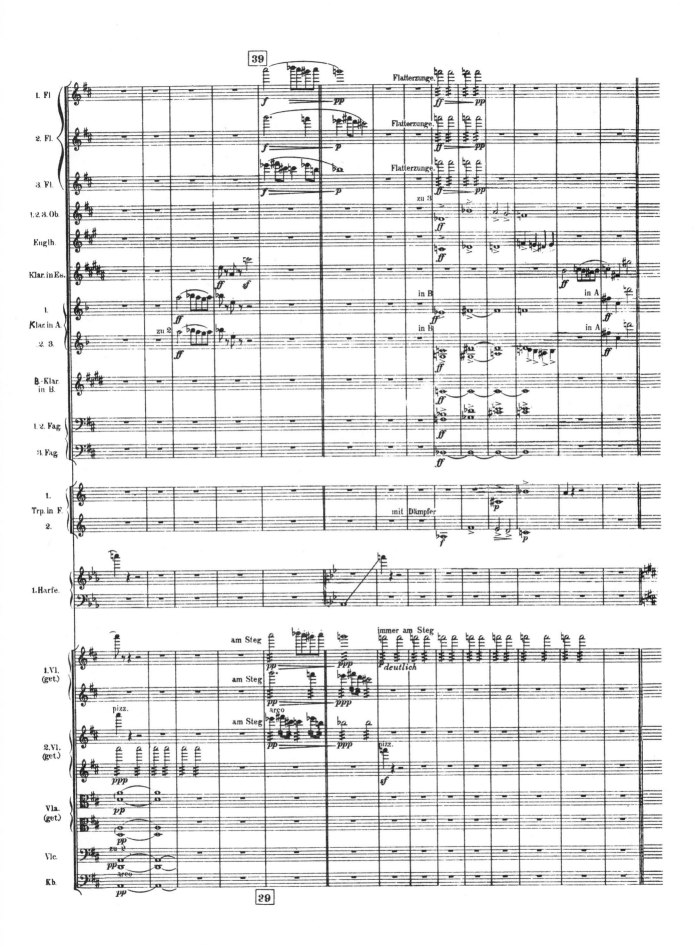

IV. Adagio.

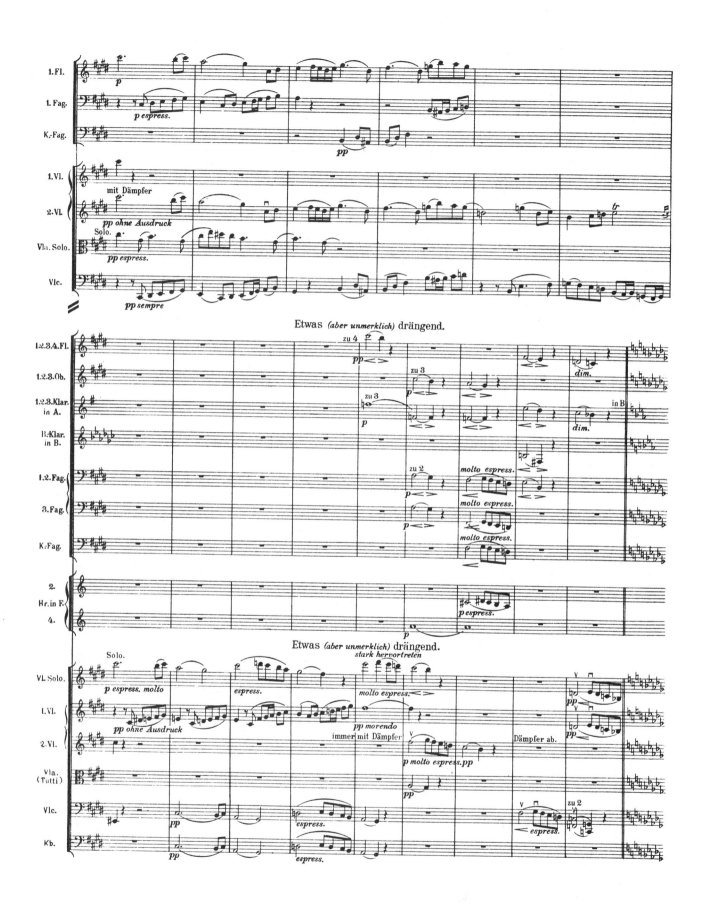

Etwas *(aber unmerklich)* drängend.

166   Symphony No. 9 (IV)

*) Die Teilung so, daß die vorderen Pulte die erste und die hinteren die zweite Stimme übernehmen.
*) Divided so that the stands in front play the first part; those further back, the second.